BECAUSE I AM THE SHORE I WANT TO BE THE SEA

BECAUSE I AM THE SHORE I WANT TO BE THE SEA

[RENÉE ASHLEY]

SUBITO PRESS 2013

ISBN: 978-0-9831150-8-3

Design & typesetting by HR Hegnauer | hrhegnauer.com
Text typeset in Garamond.

Cover art by Win Zibeon
    Detail of *Riptide* © 2008
    Synthetic Polymer on Shaped Canvas, 8" x 10"
    In private collection

Subito Press
Department of English
University of Colorado at Boulder
226 UCB
Boulder, CO 80309-0226
subitopress.org

Distributed by Small Press Distribution
1341 Seventh Street
Berkeley, California 94710
spdbooks.org

Generous funding for this publication has been provided by the
Creative Writing Program in the Department of English and the
Innovative Seed Grant Program at the University of Colorado
at Boulder.

[contemplation within the framework of the dream]

Consider the custom of likeness or unlikeness fit as the moon to a sky: let one point light up let it be relative to that The speed of that Let something quite real cry out—the dead still insisting still making themselves known their bodies ill-fit and mostly self-inflicted They change the story A pattern of escalation Of furthering and backing off Embellishment! There is no space big enough for me to speak into about this Any little human thing might act as balm What's your confession?

[bodies in increments bodies in wholes]

We are close to listening and these are stories out of
what is At the entry to day and night my darling says *the
dead are always bringing up the past* and *every view is just one
view* Before me the twins were aborted For me the dog
was put down The rabbit was stew Hard not to wager
abstraction after that Not blame but a six-pack of
consequence of recognition I say observation dilutes
image It must I can do no more than this We are the
indefinite article

[essay on observation]

The crows gather low in the trees at the woodland's edge barking their throaty wisdoms unsettling their flared black wings Squirrels hurry to gather beneath their shade just before—against gravity—they stream back upward nearer the pending havoc The deer and the bear have gone The woodchuck The poor creeping vole The crippled chipmunk gone back to his rock wall for his short life The toads are hiding beneath their stones the air is violet with what hasn't yet arrived Brown dog and black dog are crazy-eyed and lather-tongued thunder barreling from the west and flat against the neighbor's bouldered rampart is someone's yellow cat nearly dwarfed by the cowbird rigid in its mouth—not struck but stunned by that first galvanic flash so near it appears to have cut her joy in two The air swells is nickel then silver with rain—soon white with a downpour that beats the caladiums into the earth Rose of Sharon onto its knees A whole world coming down onto the world

[once quickly (quietly)]

The rough black sky then the lid of morning opens
There's a pure yellow light buried in the toad's eye
and the mute swan's plodding through shallow water
The snake is dangling from his myrtle tree and the sun
rests—curled like a gilded cat—on the ledge of the sky
The wild collation begins again Moon and the syntax of
stars The turning on their silver pivots But the blades
overhead are dividing the air And the light remains whole
despite that There can be nothing ordinary about the
ordinary Monstrous when the dark thing takes its place
Then approaching that one grain of joy on the tongue:
that place of beginning of all things able to climb the
ladder named *Assumption* And all that was dead is dead
again The horrible dreams return We are the restless
unloveliest animal Hours of penitence Hours of rain
like a beating Two instants of holy permutation Things
come to you and you use them

[the way light can travel through the center of light]

You talk then you talk self-evident and the arguments:
name ten things you most: apricots kumquats dog-love
which is just one thing reason the river flowing with
sunset forgiveness a small book about a clear bright
morsel of incautious thought joy undivided and more
of the beautiful same more of the same so much wound
and spoil you needed just a wink a cipher a shabby
little couch a howl which is all very beggar and moon
so beehive and a glittering omnium-gatherum both
syntax and point-blank disclosing those ladder-deep
ties: you're an upshot an afterclap a bringing-to-an-end
you're a harrow and a heart's-ease though you're angry
and sorry and only just starting to know

[whose bright examining]

You go anyway so What do they call you? chucklehead?
dickbender? bowl of fish? skeet? (At this rate the
woman will never ah! she's forgotten the beginning the
end) They drew a chalk shadow in the shape of the
female not the dog Head hanging like a flag (You have
to say what you think no you don't you never have to
say that out loud) Not one shifts an impulse onto the
bright with her in mind (One makes a soft simple sound
in the creak of the attic roof In the sink spilling over)
Such mewing and crying Love makes you stupid you
still don't get it you are not the world you're barely there
So The light on those gravestones still takes the shape
of gravestones and the dog whispers (the dog *never*)
bone of the center Bone of the grass God! (How can
you understand? You carry the living The heart laboring
hard in its cell Mother of all things unfruitful Victim
of everything)

[I have a theory about reflection]

I cannot put my mother in the freezer and neither can I store her in the attic nor in the bank box nor in the canister of sugar In fact she is calling me now she is ringing in my kitchen in both bedrooms in the upstairs office I am wearing her like a too-big coat The coat is made of wire I shoo her away I flap my hands: *go away go away* I am a match and every time we speak—and sometimes when we do not—she strikes me Even in the bend of a spoon I can see her reaching

[nothing less than less than nothing]

You have forgotten the words you need to say that (You've misplaced articles—things are dangling things are running on Your restrictive clause is on the rails in a universe parallel & sadly contracted) Your madmen are useless (You liked me best when I could not speak) Your friends say they're deaf—and the ringing in your ears is real You've bum-rushed everyone who's tried to love you (They tend to leave in the most abrupt ways) You're alone because you scoured your house with sorrow Your daily word is *cry* (Words have never had meaning until now) Write your rebuke in the white space around you in what could be called *sleep* or *that-which-is-like* the saying of what might really matter of what so surely you will never say at all

[and taken]

A backward breath into lung and recall: I know what
damage is I know the gun: trigger of the heart Respire
Expire Aback or away The day has been all eyes and all
those open You are in me like too many mouths

[because we are tied to the earth in this way]

Even the woodchuck swimming in his belly fat who's
taking down the pea vines and the peas the beans and
the squash is dear in the later light when all things lose
their grip on the sun A deer—blue morning glories
dying between her teeth—keeps one eye on her fawn
still with his spots woefully unafraid who eyes the
last of the bloom-shot hostas and is off on his way
towards forsythia the ropes of keria and those shade
lilies jaundiced and slug-laced Below the turning maples
slides a thready stream the color of both deep shade
and a lingering light—beneath the stream leaves fallen
and singing to the fishes who have fled that lessening
place Nothing leaves this world without somehow
breaking without sharing itself over again All of that
which we call *beauty* will change—the splitting perhaps
the tearing down we call so often *dissolution* I prefer a
love dependable as the fact of unknowing That simple
That comprehensible And words with which to stake
my ground: as quickened as a spring my story that basic
that unmistakably clear Long absences we sometimes
write down as *love* But not my kind of love Not mine

[allegory of the myth of the seemingly complex only]

Because it's on your mind: cowlick of moon bright
spittle that swings at the lip of an easy and night the
dark thing that stares past you elegant equipoise and
the unwagered self—oh what would the truth have
been? (She carried the Drowned Man in a paper sack
the Hanged Man in a cardboard cup there's a lantern
in her throat a length of twine a bolt) Oh there must
be order so blessed be each puzzle-breaker doll-shaker
trouble-taker cake-baker thing-beyond-sorrow that falls
like dust from the beams (She put a little tuxedo—no
sleeves—on his dick like dressing a thumb for the ball)
Or the story of might have happened sordid history of
the pelvic boat the furnace great well of everything (she
forgets her life half-lived down a crap-strewn road one
mile or two away lit by a spit of stars) of tell me how to
read this poem Absolutely has (Her hand the troubled
weathers) Ah Must be a principle of progression A
rubric of simplicity

[facticities, etc.]

She was born
She was born and the hospital fell into a crack where it burned
Then there was no proof she'd been born but there she was
The parents were old One was older
One was drunk One was mad And angry
Now one is dead and there's a story to that
And one is not and there's a story there too
She began writing
She began writing about what she did not know And she found out
Again there was no proof but there she was
One parent read the writing and cried ...*Nothing I could do*
One parent said *If it hadn't been for we could have Different* the parent said
She discovered she knew more She thought more She thought differently
She wrote about what she did not remember And she sometimes remembered
Somewhere in all that five dogs died And a budgie Two turtles
She can't count the cats
Somewhere in all that she married And married again
She married one who stole and one who drank Who was older Who was angry
She said *I know this story* He said *You have no proof*
He was right of course He was more often wrong but in that he was right
She writes the bone now She writes the brain She says *You were right*
She writes *If I can stay alive*
She says *How long we must
stay alive*

[where does the mind go when it refuses to leave]

You had thought of something Then that too was gone
A dark involution took its place The shed skin of a snake
Too bad: the twins flushed away Too bad the husband
soaked in wine—so sad the soddened husband And the
girl too Homely as a wasp's nest Head in a book What's
that? Dead dogs Dead brother Poor brother! Dead man
Bang bang like that Back to back Go back further Make
yourself cry Then do it again Do it every time the girl
lifts her head until she no longer lifts her head Sad the
rum grunts in all the loud nights the restaurant with
the whores upstairs You locked the white door from
the inside What were you...eight? Nine? Then all of
the above Even a new name: *Dolores* You've got no
one They all go away Poor you Poor victim of all that
occurs and all that will not before you—who has no
fault at all—go too

[there is a woman waiting for someone to tell her the truth]

There is a woman built of questions and she is broken
and there is a hole in her head the size of her mother's
head there is a hole in her head the size of her father's
wound and the dogs sniffle and fart their warm wishes
they bite they bark their huzzahs they sing there's a man
out there too and a house with dirty windows that she
loves she's not ready to swap (she's lying) the slender skill
of being alive the finite barter of staying that way

[wine not water fish not frogs]

Everything in the garden of the world the small cup
of her Gratitude and those birds pulling down the sky
What weighs most on a god's scale—other than a god?
My mother told me her first father killed her other
father I found this in a note it's my writing—she did
not tell me how Or I've forgotten again From here all I
can see is roofs but I can hear the sea Hear birds in the
inlet three doors down but the sky seems stable Such
birds appear to do no harm The question can't be *Who
will know when she's gone?* It's frogs and fishes It's atumble
askew atip in the midden I've learned not to find truth
in a world I'm trying to go on

[she thinks about the shapes things take]

She is her own apple her own various worm and wax
She is easily distracted The obligatory head-shake—
it's like when Hockney paints a chair you've got to walk
around a chair It could be chair canted in no particular
The idea you see is a place the logic of what had to
be done Not aleatoric but divined *This There That* We
become the same eye and there are more than two
horizons in the mimical world In its rousing absences
The space between us and the meaning the mind makes
All the lyric complications of stile splat seat rung and
rail Everything after a while

[a gun is not discursive]

(This time) it is a woman who lies it is the woman who
last night said *You are safe with me I do not lie* In a darkened
room such light can take out your eyes The heart's box
is broken Fib as big as an apple down your throat and
the spine's tree heating up hope's rondo spinning in
your brain Silly you No one's endearment is tidy The
garden? A huge dried-up lot And the body grateful for
unlikely waters

[black snake]

This time when the dry myrtle rustles it's the trailing
third of an indigo black snake thick as three fingers
the terror-making tip of its blue-black tail making its
way away Even so for two days everything's a snake:
thin cuff of my pants sweeping my ankle small twig
I blindly kick aside A towel I toss to the floor is snake
haven Drawer of panties Shoe My ragged bag of books
Rumor is the woman next door looked up: the black
snake dangled from a tree She must have been in a
garden like the first garden Without fear But fear is like
bread: essential Begotten and braided in the human
rope How can we face that without alarm We can't hear
it coming not the beat itself—only what it touches what
shudders at its touch Totem of ruin Our history in a
length of goddamned meat

[we are weaving the beginning on the loom of everything]

She falls down in her hours each thread a fire & there's
an air of a more vagrant fallenness inside (her griefs
withdrawn) She's become the room inside the room
things in the distance look bluer they hover in the
hospitable air & the angels of I-Thought-It-Would-Be-
Otherwise & I-Never-Thought-At-All have affixed the
small countries of their wings—though neither knows
a feather from a flame—so that trees move aside &
the wind blows too fast past the bolted windows (You
cannot be your own regret) Listen: we invent things
when facts are insufficient We weave the beginning on
the loom of everything pick up those branches that the
wind took down & the moon's full-up with exit wounds
& inertia (of quiescence & a structure reminiscent of
turbulent equations) All hours are not equal in this that
we find is neither one thing nor another When the
message leaves the body we do this to live I'm telling
only you the world's ablaze with foreboding & all that
is at rest (yes) Still gesture's a part of our mistakable say

[say this]

And sometimes there may be good reason for such
quaint perfidy—a molar cracking a jawbone wrestled
from its pinion and groove the daily grounds for misery
sticking in your pipes One more day of quotidian rustle
of the how-it-must-be-at-this-juncture despite you with
your hands in the mean one's fur The air around you
senescence-heavy and perfumed with boiled fish All
good things are accidents: the hook at the end of your
personal crook the bleat of the lambish thing inside you
is one more good dark Read the books! See? All our
shapings coincide with the beautiful equation In our
drowse we turn and turn three times to press down the
bed Then two times more for our bum luck The seven
vertebrae in our necks relax our impossible thumbs
curl as if around something and there are six feet as I
understand it in the grave Numbers cause such history
If you can count it's already past All prophecy is luck or
sense Two beats more than you can dance to All luck is
dumb All sight is always skewed *Wag* and *Scoundrel! Piss*
and *Ant* are the names you know you know Listen: all
day you count the pennies in your brain loose change
Loose cannon Loose ends lost dog *Old Ninny Fusspot
Layabout Bastard Partaker-of-Bread* What say you *Thumb-
sucker Bitch-in-Heat* Say this poor *Outlaw Bayer-in-the-
Night*: don't bargain for history or naming Don't count
on what you thought you thought or what you think
you have to say *Say this*

[experience]

You stuff envelopes You sit kids You hate kids Your
tongue's stuck to your lip You taste glue all the time
and kid snot's on your fingers You'd rather read a book
rather be lost in some world that isn't this one Rather
be grown-up and make money enough to run away or at
least go skating or to the movies with a friend You have
no friends You don't talk on the telephone You drew one
on the wall in your room You call No one answers you

.

Burger burger rootbeer floats and fries Inside on the
grill outside hopping cars *What can I get you ma'am?*
But damn it's a man and nobody's happy now Then
you get paid in pennies to boot At nine you're done
You have a date but you're stood up again It is love
but not for him You're fifty-eight now and still think
of that boy's blue-green car and his soft hands At least
he pretends to cry when he dumps you You're still
grateful for his gentleness

.

You're in retail You sell Christmas balls to old ladies
who drive you nuts You hate their assumption that balls
and tinsel are your only life Who knows what country
tinsel comes from? Not me Read the damn box you old

bat You've got a line a mile long you're at the register and the credit cards are holding up the works Sign on the line Mrs. Furbelow not across the slip where the prices are Put your glasses on! You don't last there long

.

You work the eight-to-five in the courthouse print shop the presses running hard the thump-thump-thump of the clamped drum clogging up your dreams at night At six a.m. you're toast You're exhausted You're drunk on sleeplessness You're fucked Probably printed the ticket yourself that you got at lunch for crossing those double yellow lines in your car The whole world is wrong You should be in school reading Proust or Joyce You should be on your fat ass not your aching feet

.

You pump gas You're good but you're not sexy and the stations with the sexy girls get all the boys But you can smile and talk how-de-doo with the old men in Plymouths who are too frightened of their gray wives to buy gas at the titty stations Your boyfriend owns this Shell He's younger than you and he didn't go to college but he's smart You're working on your thesis at night: *Courtly Love as Archetype* and by the time you're done he throws you out

.

Every every everyone's assistant Typing Copying
Finding the primary sources The phone is ringing It's
her aunt It's his wife or daughter It's the office: where's
the goddamn teacher? You can't say She's stuck in
traffic He's boffing the blonde in his nine a.m. class
somewhere on the coast in a cheesy hotel Sand in the
sheets Lamp shade broken You know You've been
there He'll be back by quarter past four if he doesn't
have to stop for gas

.

On the other side of town you ghostwrite for a woman
who goes to the park with her big black dog then takes
two naps while you put in your eight or ten hours then
take the goddamned work home because she gives
it to you just two weeks before it's due One grand a
book is what you get She gets fifteen times that at least
You're getting screwed but it's experience You're owed
three thousand The check's no good She's out of town
You tell the husband *I'll burn your fucking house down*

.

The scientists are smarter than you are but you can
spell You type their white papers their letters their
requisitions You teach them where the commas go
They can spell *gasification* but not *their* They're amazing
You love them all but one the slimy one the sleazy one
who offers you money to go home with him You are

appalled You shouldn't have joked when he pulled out that wad of bills at the luncheon Shouldn't have said *I'll go home with him*

.

You've dusted battleship filters You've cut cheese You've translated French badly Transcribed inaudible audio tapes Mowed lawns Sold books And you worked a switchboard—the old kind: woven cords and metal plugs You've walked dogs—and OK you've kissed some crazy ass You've been a poetry whore (that's a metaphor) You've taught fiction but this isn't it You pull it all in It makes you You You say: *There's some sort of lesson in this a story of some kind*

[my father is ashes]

We are electric I know our conductor He is a very sad man We are not in a field of cosmos We are not in a field I'm only telling you that when the message leaves the body I do not know what to make of the world I make you up from the little I know with almost with soon Is it possible the thing I love most is guilt or that you are gone? We are such pain and we are utterance We are a strange thing in the air You are so imperfectly dead

[you]

think you own your days and that you're fine but ghosts
and DNA know how to find you The dead will pick
your pockets every time You've argued and you've lost
Now you're resigned to finding in your daily bread the
traits of one who led you to believe you owned your life
and thought that fine But you cannot win a war against
the dead You can't decline to dream your dreams You're
screwed and can't unscrew It's nothing new: your dead
will pick your pockets every time So you settle for those
hours when angry bloodlines and the hungry ghosts
seem absent from your view: they let you think you
own your hours That's fine and almost dandy but then
something nasty and malign will lift its head and you're
left knowing that it's true: the dead have picked your
pockets one more time So you pretend to welcome
them: you build a shrine You give up knowing what
you thought you knew: that you have to own your days
and will be fine Until you're dead—and maybe after—
damned dead will pick your pockets every time

[neither the cock on fire nor the tin roof banging]

And that is not the barking of pigs you hear The spleen-angels are wrangling in the garden again Listen There's no need for upset It's what they do what they are best at The angels are experts Are doing their job Trust them— I know it's hard to see And the brouhaha stops you Not even drunks caterwaul like that Feral critters have better manners So walk past first then turn Look over your shoulder The light is better that way You'll have to listen past the growling The angels are calling your name They know what you're dreaming They're sitting at your table They're wearing your cast-off shoes

[I run to the sad man in the white car and]

This is a different gun reader than you have heard about
before From me This is a different tragedy The man
in the white car is weary of sorrow weary the way a
woman becomes weary of a man Or of her life (or of a
satchel which might contain the whole history a whole
of sorrow's vestige) This man is learning the gun: singed
wing orphan rare bird Sorrow can fly and a gun can
fly and a shot And time But time is simply a metaphor
here & hardly a metaphor at all Not flying Dragging a
busted wing dragging its bitter (like a satchel) Dragging
its stark and dragging its bleak dragging its heavy its
carcass its blasted-out carrion heart

[mostly there is mostly I do]

i

To live you must row across the mother How
good it is to go away how good not to go back
again Imagine the air around a bell how it is
displaced the way the city sets a fire in the sky
and burns Imagine the heart folded like a bedsheet
Her glass letters Everything grounded in the pelvic
boat: our lady of the pipe dream lady of perpetual
disappointment The landscape of ropes in the blue
story twinning and taking her the dark way home—
a life stacked like wood the uninfinite self still
by itself with the unfounded rumors of simplicity

ii

You can't even count the times you've told the story:
the father the sound of no response at all the white car
and then racing the ambulance home No sea to cross
for the father no trope to carry his body back to the husk
of a house in the mountains Just the gun the blossom
of red above his ear Undertakers who do a piss-poor job
the bared head seeping on the satin A sea of nothing but
minus while the skull hollows itself And regret having
petals Or as well an ocean's worth of recognition: lights
out water running a not-quite-on-the-mark precipitous blast
Your grandmother's name was Crick No relation And what

iii

is relation anyway? Blood running through a corridor
A swinging gate You will die but you hope not drown
or burn You hope sleep takes you with your laundry done
You hope your shame—big as a mountain top—dies with
you that it doesn't rest visible and polished on the mantel
like a loving cup or small casket of ash with a plaque
of belonging You don't know who you are but for that
small thing only you will name—and you would not pass
that on You have been careful not to pass that on You
throw the windows open the doors toss the drapes out
batter the rugs You hope the wind will clean your house

[an art like any other]

Take a woman who has no child and give her a child—
like that!—and she thinks: *more than me more than all of
you* It's beautiful But of course it doesn't happen that
way You never wanted it to happen that way You know
your heart is a mistake You are the woman bringing
nothing driving in the semiotic fog The city is wearing
its shroud: you are an elephant a pearl You are as right
as a gate You are hidden in your bone nest when you
hear it: a young man restless at an intersection speaking
to a silver phone: *No no Not embarrassed* he says *I just
didn't want to wake up next to you* He's not speaking to
you you're thankful for that Because you know when
he says *I love you* her heart closes—bam!—like a window
falling shut She says her heart is not a window it is a
store and the store is closed And nobody knows how
the heart stores what it knows We know the other truth
We know the sky is frayed and that the beginning begins
here Every time the body has its say: *I can do that for you*
It says *You are building the mountain you fall from* And you
are undone in the air It says *An art like any other* There
must be a word for this but you do not have a speaking
part Because you are not the same as before Because no
one was at hand to say *Please don't go*

[look]

There's sorrow wrapped up in an old woman & over there: rage in a man who is trying the sea on like a sharkskin suit Above both the sky is an upturned bowl of birds & a vague history's settling like mist on the place where the bones hatch So many pities There was a man with a separate discontent he was feeding the squirrels he was feeding the deer What a woman took from him was not quite the heart We are outsiders everywhere—not just in art—& the limits of language don't hinder us As if we could speak to *abstraction* or *fact* Always this way alone among the others The slabber & drool of our dogs in the dark & more light than we can know than the cowl of the pitiful moon can shed Plenty to read by Just look over there: the robin's red breast has burst & her heart flown out The sun's strong fire turns our own skin to spite The house is still in flames I'm telling you now so you'll know: light is leaping from our roof Our own books are burning

[some of the things I thought I saw]

(as if yes as if no) – (as) something
I'm not cooking's boiling over:

    the green roiling aura above my sleeping father
      meat that bled all summer
    the metaphor that fell from the table
      mouthful of bones ear full of bees

(the thread that held everything) (the many
                verbs of desiring)

(of all things unenlightened and enduring)

    the name of that rose that grew so well near the sea
    sheet after sheet of the white-edged sea
    (the sun just an old man's rag)
      (a furious flight of starling and angel)
    pearl from the flesh

the *oh* and the *oh*!
(in light of the complex:)

    and body as poorbox
(spunk and spittle, spirit and poop
a nod to the conflagration
a poor attempt to piss past the flames)

and the woman who loved like nails and glue
(: night's throat coarse as split wood)

that sputtering at the tongue's root

(enough sorrow to fill your hat and a wind to take it away)   '

then too the too-sweet alyssum the poppy pod the glassful of winking red juice

(once quietly once quickly:)

some of the things I thought (I thought) I saw

    sparrows dancing in the sparrow-deep grass
    and a hunter's moon watering each

[intensity for beginners]

The fox is as red as the dog is white and my friend Mary
cuts the balls on sheep I swear The words should be
as simple as the mind is not *In tent cities* For example:
disjunction of the beaten heart: enough sparrows for
a quorum and at least one time in another country a
young boy was chained inside a grain bin I heard this
Don't explain But go on The poet John Kinsella was
struck by lightning twice he swears He was a child then
I believe him *Ten pests in a teak cup The art is a homely
punter* Now a faggot of small hearts is set afire—the
shadows that would throw! Pray for the divided hooves
of deer for the thick stinking fur of bears For unseating
the heart of loneliness For compost And shit in deep
mounds Pray for the tufts of titmice For the bull
running both ways at once For magnitude Except for
every thing we're interchangeable: there was no dog
there but a shadow of that dog in the deeper shade

[what is visible is what mostly is]

So this too is no longer a poem about the bat in the opera
house and not that other one either Nothing *Fleder*-
Nothing -*maus* Not the brown one in the roof beams
spreading its fingery wings not the long-handled net we
catch it in What is visible is what mostly is A relic one
small figment of fractured bone No thing is holy or ever
will be Look: some of all the ways you could get caught:
water under water or the earth beneath all that

[because I am the shore I want to be the sea]

i

But you too know this: the wanting to be what you
cannot—except by extension—and the bearing of
those secrets so immeasurable not even an ocean can
conceal them And in the ocean's failure the mountain
shows its hard side its watershed steep with its varied
waves of not-sea its gravities and declivities its runnels
its hummings and echoes vaulting against the inner ear
a passel of unruly birds against a pearled tympan even
at the pan-flat center of the smaller world where time
takes its man-made dip and leans towards the west as
here on our eastern brink we lean towards the west and
what we can prove we are: a little snatch of fatty meat or
more some water a rakeful of invisible wrack a faggot of
bones and what you suspect—a far more interpretable
sea—sticks and stones a little salt-worn glass

ii

And there's your figment of the whale-tinctured sea
figment of the great green of want of the lift and drop
the necessary grains beneath and between So you throw
something anything into the water and it reminds you of
a story which recalls for you a scene The green becomes
the cover on his taut-made bed and he is sleeping there
atop the soft chenille The white sheets pulled tight
beneath He is fully clothed He is fetal when he sleeps
one hand above and one hand below the undressed
pillow that buoys his head up as another smaller one
will later when the bullet's entrance still seeps and a
pillow is entrusted with both the head and the hole—
like a keepsake—but for now you dare not wake him
he is peacefully asleep and with any luck at all unaware
of what gets tangled every waking hour on the slim sea
ropes of his genes And the little snow there is arrives at
an angle to the sea tripping on the wave of his upturned
hip the bone there and that white is not the cloud tips
topping the strand but the fallout of a great tenderness
and for that sleep is known to be a smaller decease like
the bottle like the many like the going away again to
catch his breath and then coming back again For him it
was all like drowning

iii

Then the paper sea And your dream of the paper sea You have kept his notes and *Evangeline* and your friend Stv. said *Funny* Stv. said to you *It's afternoon here and you're in a later time zone there Write a poem about that please* but so far not a bit of luck Though you thought and thought and not far from here there are starlings falling through an abandoned sky iridescent commas with beaks and feet What can that possibly mean? They've been downed in the colorless air The farmers are nodding The cattle are showing their spines The chickens their tumbling stones Those starlings are striking the earth like clods of dark earth The dead should not be allowed to rain Don't read the daily news Too much found in the cogent sheets so far from the reasonable sea Not like the sun stench of sea wrack not like sea rope at your ankles with the gasses swelling There is no time zone where he will be sleeping and sleeping and not going down

iv

And it all spills over you the one who did not save
you and her gate-leg of blindness You swear she can
breathe under water and yet she is blameless You have
always understood the argument of the thorny spine
narrow sea of glass wed to the not-glass toughened
and determinedly not seeing Sea of hours Sea of never
saying or of saying it to the wall that would hold back
the sea The world is encoded indelible with *lonely* and
sorry with *no* with *please* with *no that never happened* Sea
of not-knowing and unknowing both There is water
all around now but you came from the pan-flat center
of the smaller world where the blackbirds gyred in the
niveous blue and the sky was the only sea You did not
choose to be pulled down You were so far west there
was no west left and still See How could you ever have
known You never in all your life could have known

v

that there are other deeps spotted from the brink
of the mountain the what you did or did not do or
turned to or have become What you want is what you
want unpoetic simple—raw meat—and then there is
the riptide A body in the swift green valley is burning
while another to its west is overcome by what would
put out the flames Time is heating up and travels at all
speeds in all directions Stv. said *You're in a later time zone
there* Please How much later can it get? It pulls from
the breakers a wail guttural grave vibration and wave
pressing the body back so the body falls this one more
time wanting over and again wanting not to want and
will die complaining and in want of just catching that
last unfathomable breath

[while I still have you]

There's that stuff about death: the stiff then soft thing
the fatty soup that blends with gravel and pit the body's
stew slug slime and bother—the long messy wait (do you
believe that anymore?) for resurrection and for anger to
disperse with the prions with the thin digested stomach's
walls the nuclei of the heart's cells—those jails we throw
ourselves into Yes No No Yes again: the broom whip
the pitiful scourge Accusation Attribution The thing I
forgot to say the O the *you* the *While you're here you just
might listen?* As though we were both living still

[how to put it]

The fragment as spoken by the one lost His heart singing in its dish
The dish breaking beneath his heart's singing Down by the reservoir
cars slide into the darkening water The moon's pull does not save them
In daylight in the parking lot of the market three miles away the gray birds
will not move for the car the one-legged birds stand on their one leg
The world is not broken The world is local Singing in its spinning dish

[OK we'll call it a vessel]

Let's call the heart *a stone* No we've used up *heart* and *stone*... So *vessel* it is and it breaks And it sorries It moon it bale Hey says vessel I want out want stop Want the endless nothing and everything too Vessel is too hard Is multiple And laden Defers to the chain of mentally and bodily—pipes all over the ark are breaking Vessel in your sealed vessel now what will you do?

[all my suicides have been men]

It's no one's bed we're lying in & from it we can hear the almost-ocean in the eaves of the house behind the other house There is the whisper intrusion makes There the four low steps *Here Rest yourself before* There the cherry plum its red-black leaves sweeping the green roof The incense of sweet pea climbs the trellis You had the gun You the belt The belt! & the cliff face took you middle boy You left & I do not pretend to gainsay blame The sky was deep blue tulle & there were other skies but I was my center Always I am my center & everywhere the ghost text appears in waves in sheets in trifles of thought no longer than a trifle's worth I claim to be changed Come back I am grown I know nothing now & am willing to tell you

[consider this world in all its blue extremities]

She's spoken too often of waves like those & of one
man dying—now again the world is made of rain &
of a dark too entirely visible—absurd to list one's
sorrows like wants or like symptoms: there are limits
to a language stacked like that—the mystery's still half-
hearted & stars remain just small pricks of absence in an
otherwise unlit sky: the perfect moon's light is spinning
in the dogwoods—the slumbery pond's being choked
by the beautiful lilies—there is so much to grieve for
it has never been easy grieving in this world—& this
is how one small poem unfolds in her long *Book of
Difficulty*—she has the notion every instant should be
reconsidered That pain's just a reliquary—that each
sudden moment should be perceived & praised as blue

[the attic room]

This is the place (where nothing is deft or quite complete) to contemplate a love like the one which did not exist but that you hoped might make you new again the one from which you couldn't fail to fall from lightly But look around Each thing here could be anywhere in anyone's dusty upstairs room What you cannot find is always the same what you manage somehow to figure out consistently pedestrian—each solid knock and trunkful trade-offable and special only because you call it yours What should have been—you call it *should* It's just sky blue sky—immaterial mutable so vast it's not even really there

[café des quatre vents]

It's only a postcard Nothing about the wind knocking debris to the curb No hint about the heart We are the act of consequence—figure and profile Everything is fatal and we suffer the world and its waters Somebody will always object and we grieve for those living hard amidst these shifting miracles Right now is when I love you That world is only darkness Our place is in those small lights It's best to be clear

[not too far from Coosawatchie]

Too easy to ask where is the boy Too easy the four
walls of rain with thunder for a roof Too hard the
earth The life spins and this is the room and this is
the window Over there little calves lying down and the
green fields waving Over there so much sand it looks
like water And there is water That swale is a woman's
thigh We have these common texts and our pointless
tasks Absurd Such philosophy! Derisible Two shoes
lined up like feet at the side of the road Little sayings
to get you through the weather this close to the edge
of some inchoate world

[armadillo]

Deep in the unlit palm scrub a rustling wedded to
the ground and you with your sorry light searching
Armadillo half-blind not yet stupid with fear tough-
skinned like your heart which whispers through its sack
at the sight of you *I am small and unlikely myself* This
is about what you cannot know It's about the other
who is beautiful and a god if there can be a god You
have many questions If you find you must speak please
swear you'll turn your light off You can ask about the
world but do it softly

[how to see it]

Dark traffic & plenty Rte 206 Four north-bound lanes
& a breast-high divider poured from powdered rock
Eyes of a large doe in one car's lights How the world
slows them wide as black moons leaping to the hood
then up the windscreen's steeper angle & into space—
where it happens—then hard to the killing highway
where she spins like a dish on a stick The black air had
been transparent Now thick with her light broken free
A deer made of bright Our useless sorry & cry our
metaphors mixed: constellated wasted bird-brained &
tongue-tied

[some man made this bridge]

At this rate the woman will never cross the bridge The
fog dense as hope could ease her heart from her chest
and send her reeling Blind water would rise to study
her body her dark hair rippling her cheeks a moist
shade of cut pear She's ripe with trembling but has
forgotten which way she should go She should have
turned around she thinks Each breath takes a cloud of
unknowing The fog tucks her in She with no sense at
all of its genius or of taking a fall

[the verbs of desiring]

How tired the self is of self, its earth twirling in the air and not-air and I
know a woman who ate only bread until she died of bread

Oh the where-
is-she-now Which is not a question Which is a noun of circumstance And
disquietude: lovely word And *hairsbreadth Stupor mundi Kettle-of-fish-
that-turned-your-heart*

You are returning from an alphabet ransacked
by thirst by the gamut of implication neatly sung: a tongue that speaks
body A punctuated earth You who are resolute of hungry brutes and
fooled by the beggar's bowl of moon and tide of scat of pellet and flop
—and the body's dead end is an assured apostrophe

There are more ways
to mean than you can make note of

Look! Something is pretty in the sky
—it might just be the sky—though installation's been askant Or what it sits
upon is opposed to the level eye A panoply of possibilities—all those bears
pirouetting in your penthouse!

Oh if it or they were only Or if you And or if I

[a wind is like so many arrows
a house like so many some kind of doors]

It's more complicated than that Metaphor or not it's
this one body breaking up sends the mind's bear scram-
bling in the pit Self is a rugged low-down thing Time's
loaded Poor mind Poor bear Poorest hour of end The
winds are up: foreclosures Every place you look eye-
sore and bellyflop the single imperfect discourse of an
unfinished world

[bless]

Bless the susurration of gratitude and the breath taken
in and again taken The rat-tailed shudder: the face
in the pond Pray for the solitary who have no model
pray for the models of those who do (each one having
shown the open and close) Bless those of the rope And
the gun And the gas The pill-takers and skin-breakers
Bless the cliff one man drove over Bless the knife that
wouldn't cut and the one that did Bless the train that
didn't come And the one that will come soon

[oh yes tomorrow expect the ordinary]

The dogs sing beautifully over everything beautiful or
not—white sleet or white sun—and you have never yet
begun with nothing Tell your friends to wait This will
take some time Imagine a burned house—steamy sill
dampened ash Shingle lintel coal An emptiness spread
like soot Can you even begin to comprehend *nothing?*
Posit a negative in a positive mind the idea of no idea
expanding? The dark smell of *gone* of *you can't get this
back* Consider the stark break between *yes* and *so often*—
between *no* and *not yet some time* Think *hypothetical absolute*
Oh druggery! Oh *get me through this* Every day dog song
and dander jig your approach—such joy! Privilege
and you so heart-poor A poverty of fire You yourself
consumed But not so simple Never as clear as that
Nothing so sweetly entire

[utterance and origin]

She opens *Her Book of Difficulty* and reads *nor tomorrow*
and *her flock of voices* and she listens So wise to And hears
an array of and *how many beginnings* She reads *five further
findings* and the eyelid of the sky flickers The horizon
lowers What was sky becomes embankment Then
another token the token *blue* And ah There it is: *can't
figure it out* and *evidence to the contrary* She continues: *the
remaining terrible things* She grieves for the living Remorse
for the dead and is shamed again all over again Neither
one will be resolved Her eyes fall closed Twin blinds
Twin shutters Blank walls on the inside She repeats: *You
must come to love one thing*

About the Author

Renée Ashley is the author of four previous volumes of poetry (*Salt*—Brittingham Prize in Poetry, Univ. of Wisconsin Press; *The Various Reasons of Light*; *The Revisionist's Dream*; *Basic Heart*—X. J. Kennedy Poetry Prize, Texas Review Press) and two poetry chapbooks, *The Museum of Lost Wings* and *The Verbs of Desiring*, as well as a novel, *Someplace Like This*. She is on the faculty of Fairleigh Dickinson University's two low-residency graduate programs, the MFA in Creative Writing and the MA in Creative Writing and Literature for Educators. She has received fellowships in both poetry and prose from the New Jersey State Council on the Arts and a fellowship in poetry from the National Endowment of the Arts.

Acknowledgments

With gratitude to David and Noni Diamantopoulos for allowing me to hide out at the Hide Out, and with big fat love to Jack Pirkey, Barney, Pootie, Steven, and Mona for being where I need them to be, to Cat Doty for The Us Show; and to my dear, patient Mel Kershaw who continues to pull my parts out of the fire, I say, It's true: I need a keeper. And for the keeping, I thank you all.

Grateful acknowledgment is made to the editors of the following journals in which these poems, sometimes in earlier versions and with alternate titles, first appeared: *Big City Lit, Bomblog, Columbia, Columbia Poetry Review, Connotation Press, Crazyhorse, Edison Review, Field, Greensboro Review, The Journal of Literary Arts, Kenyon Review, The Literary Review, Mead, Poetry ETC Anthology, Schuylkill Valley Journal of the Arts, Serving House Journal, Tiferet, Verse Daily, Writers on the Job.*

[I have a theory about reflection] was awarded the The Robert Watson Literary Prize from *Greensboro Review* and a number of the poems in this manuscript were published in *The Verbs of Desiring,* winner of the new american press Chapbook Award.

About Subito Press

Subito Press is a non-profit literary publisher based in the Creative Writing Program of the Department of English at the University of Colorado at Boulder. Subito Press encourages and supports work that challenges already-accepted literary modes and devices.

Subito Press

Noah Eli Gordon, *director*
Stephen Daniel Lewis, *managing editor*
Adam Bishop
Bruce Lin
Caroline Rothnie
Chris Hutt
Kevin Kane
Logan Priess
Mark Jaskowski
Matthew Treon
Randy Prunty
Sara Renee Marshall

Subito Press Titles

2008

Little Red Riding Hood Missed the Bus by Kristin Abraham
With One's Own Eyes: Sherwood Anderson's Realities
by Sherwood Anderson
Edited and with an Introduction by Welford D. Taylor
My Untimely Death by Adam Peterson
Dear Professor, Do You Live in a Vacuum? by Nin Andrews

2009

Self-Titled Debut by Andrew Farkas
F-Stein by L.J. Moore

2010

Song & Glass by Stan Mir
Moon Is Cotton & She Laugh All Night by Tracy Debrincat
Bartleby, the Sportscaster by Ted Pelton

2011

The Body, The Rooms by Andy Frazee
Death-in-a-Box by Alta Ifland
Man Years by Sandra Doller

2012

We Have With Us Your Sky by Melanie Hubbard
Vs. Death Noises by Marcus Pactor
The Explosions by Mathias Svalina

2013

Because I Am the Sea I Want to Be the Shore by Renée Ashley
The Cucumber King of Kėdainiai by Wendell Mayo
Domestic Disturbances by Peter Grandbois